To Denis and Marlena,

Wishing you all
the best.
Enjoy!

Scott P. Jacobs
'05

THE ART OF SCOTT JACOBS

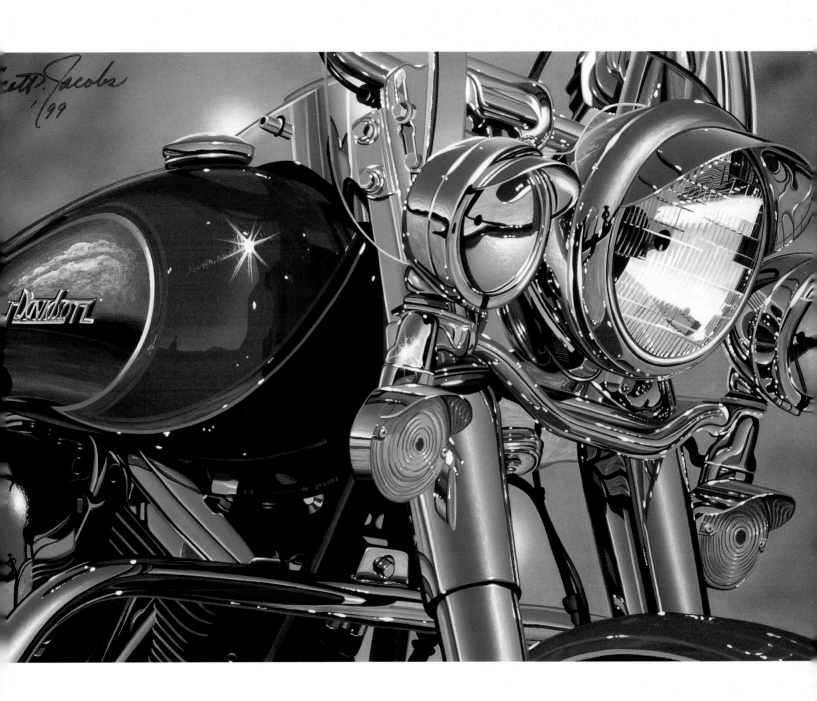

ACKNOWLEDGEMENTS

I wish to acknowledge and thank the following people for allowing me to live an artist's dream:

My wife Sharon, who gave me paints, canvas, and an easel for Christmas in 1989 to revive my interest in becoming an artist again.

My wife Sharon, who has spent many days and weeks alone while I'm touring the world promoting my work.

My wife Sharon, for being my biggest supporter and best friend.

My daughters, Olivia and Alexa, who give me one kiss on my palm for every night I'm away, with strict instructions that I take just one before I go to sleep each night.

My junior high school teacher, who noticed the drawings on my books and made me the artist for the school newspaper.

Sherry Hall and Ellen Greg, who gave me my first job in an art gallery while I was in high school and two years later, sold me that same gallery at a price below market value.

Frank Tatulli, who has done so many things for me to prevent me from hurting my hands.

Ron Copple, who in 1993 suggested that I start painting motorcycles, and I'm still painting them.

My publisher, Ron Segal of Segal Fine Art, and his staff, who have been promoting and selling my art worldwide since 1993.

My primary photographer, Jeff Hackett, who travels all over the country with me and makes it possible to work from such awesome reference photographs.

Photographers Michael Lichter and Don Rogers, who have supplied me with incredible reference photos.

Artists such as Charlie Bell, Ralph Goings, Norman Rockwell, Harold Cleworth, and Maxfield Parrish, who have inspired my style and true appreciation of art.

Artist Doug Webb, who taught me the patience it takes to be a photo-realist and that it doesn't happen overnight.

Harley-Davidson Motor Co., Chevrolet Motor Co., Hot Wheels Racing, Arlen Ness, and numerous custom bike builders, who have made machines worthy of painting.

The art galleries, museums, and dealerships that have hosted shows and displayed my work. Without supporters like you, I wouldn't have an audience.

Cliff Stieglitz and the *Airbrush Action* staff and its designers, who had the vision and patience to jump through hoops and over obstacles to see this book completed.

Cliff Stieglitz, who has been a great supporter of my career and a friend from the very beginning.

And, to everyone not mentioned who has ever purchased one of my prints or products or just enjoys and appreciates my work... I thank you!

ART DIRECTOR: Cliff Stieglitz
DESIGNER: Michele DeBlock
DESIGN CONSULTANT: Chuck Routhier
EDITORS: Cliff Stieglitz & Jennifer Bohanan
COPY EDITOR: David Mermelstein & Kathryn Priest
PRODUCTION MANAGER: Michele DeBlock
JACKET DESIGN: Roy Ritola, Inc., Jeff Kaplan, Designer

First published in the United States of America by:
    Airbrush Action, Inc.
    P.O. Box 438
    3209 Atlantic Avenue
    Allenwood, NJ 08720
    Tel: (732) 364-2111
    Fax: (732) 367-5908
    E-mail: cstieglitz@monmouth.com
    www.airbrushaction.com

ISBN: 0-9637336-2-1
Printed and bound in Singapore

CONTENTS

PREFACE

If I were to identify one particular characteristic that has carried me to this point in my artistic career, I would have to say it is patience. When young artists ask me how I became successful, I think they expect me to tell them about some special technique I've mastered, or my trademark style, or even some instinctive, mysterious "talent." I may owe my success to a little bit of each of those things, but without patience, I might have given up on my art long before it turned from an aspiration into a satisfying, lucrative profession.

Patience is not a quality I started out with; it's something I've acquired through the years. When I first started, I would try to complete a painting in two hours—now I'm up to three or four hundred hours per painting. With each new piece, I focus on trying to bring my work to a new level, because I believe that one of the keys to a being a good artist is the ability to remain a student, continually learning new things and finding ways to improve.

For as long as I can remember, I've been "into" art. When I was in school, I drew a lot and, like most kids, doodled in and on my notebooks. When the editor of my school newspaper noticed some of this notebook art, he asked me to become the paper's official artist, and I accepted. I designed a new masthead every week, changing the lettering styles and developing new images. It was fun. The work may not have been all that good, but it got me toying with paints and thinking about a career in art.

I didn't actually start out as an artist. After I finished high school, I started a traveling art gallery, working out of the back of a van. I exhibited a few artists; I built, carved, and stained the frames for their work myself. I moved from place to place, selling the work at events, such as those "starving artist" shows you may have seen advertised. When I was nineteen, I had saved enough money to take advantage of a once-in-a-lifetime opportunity to buy my own gallery.

Working as an art dealer exposed me to the mechanisms of the art world and gave me a foot in the door for my own career as an artist. I learned about the best avenues for getting exposure, how to make connections with publishers and printing companies, and why some artists seem to be more successful than others. When I started trying to develop my own painting style, someone advised me just to keep painting. He said, "if you keep painting, people will recognize your work because you're still around." He was, in effect, teaching me about the value of patience.

As a gallery owner, I was able to observe how people responded to the art that was on exhibit. I noticed how impressed they were with the photo-realistic work, so I decided to try my hand at it. I entered a photo-realistic painting of a fire truck in a local art contest and won. It was a validation of what I was trying to do, and it motivated me to keep at it.

Now, when people come to my shows, I am always blown away by their response to my work. The public is a huge inspiration to me, so I try to get out there and make appearances at galleries, Harley-Davidson dealerships, and motorcycle events as often as possible. It helps me sell paintings, like a rock band touring after its latest album, but there's more to it than that. These events energize me. After an appearance, I can't wait to go home and get back in front of the easel. I don't think I'd be as effective an artist if I didn't get out there every few weeks.

Ten years ago, I never would have believed how far I've come. My work has changed dramatically, not only in quality, but also in style. When I look back at my earlier pieces, I can see how much I've improved. I love to show those paintings to younger artists struggling to make a name for themselves, to point out that eight or nine years ago, I was there. I try to keep pounding it into their heads—you just have to be patient.

I honestly love the challenge of painting Harley-Davidson motorcycles—it's like I'm painting their history. I also paint Harleys because they sell. If you love painting and don't want it to be just a hobby, you have to be able to make money at it. In some ways, I've gotten lucky—my timing was right, and along the way I've met some great people who were willing to share their knowledge with me. In addition to tips and shortcuts, their encouragement has been invaluable, and I hope I can offer the same kind of motivation to today's budding artists.

Scott Jacobs

The Jacobs family (from left to right): Alexa, Scott, Sharon, and Olivia.

Sara Nee, photographer

ABOUT THE ARTIST

In just under a decade, Scott Jacobs has earned his place in a primarily American subculture, elevating the mysterious, often-misunderstood world of motorcycles and fast cars to the realm of fine art. With his paintings on display in 52 countries, Scott has bridged the gap between widely diverse worlds. His imagery has been reproduced as posters, mixed medias, giclées, and serigraphs, as well as appearing on merchandise, such as jigsaw puzzles, clothing, stationery, clocks, beer steins, and collector's plates.

Scott's first efforts appeared at his Westfield, New Jersey, gallery under the pseudonym "Escoteté," a clever distortion of his first name. In search of candid feedback, Scott developed the alias to get an honest critique from visitors to the gallery—few who came to view and comment on the work knew they were speaking to the artist who created it. After hearing and observing their reactions, Scott honed his craft and finally began to paint under his own name.

While at the Forbes Estate to do a portrait of Malcolm, Sr., Scott was granted access to the business tycoon's famed motorcycle collection. He painted his first Harley, *Fat Boy*, and his career producing photo-realistic renderings of Harley-Davidson motorcycles was off and running.

Since that time, Scott has continued to garner acclaim for his work, gaining momentum with each new piece. He was the first artist to be officially licensed worldwide by Harley-Davidson to produce and sell prints featuring their motorcycles. American Licensed Products, an official Harley-Davidson clothing retailer, developed a "Scott Jacobs Art to Wear" line. He is also licensed by the Chevrolet Motor Company (Corvette Division) and Mattel, Hot Wheels Race Team, working with Kyle Petty.

Scott's work has been reproduced on Franklin Mint limited-edition collector plates—his first, *Pumping Iron*, was one of the largest sellers in the company's history. American Greetings has published wall, desk, and computer calendars with Scott's images. His works have been collected by a host of celebrities, including U.S. Senator Ben Nighthorse Campbell, John Elway, Karl Malone, Dan Aykroyd, Steve Hendrickson, Arlen Ness, Michael Jackson, Willie G. Davidson, Jon Bon Jovi, and the rock groups ZZ Top, Survivor, and Loverboy.

Scott has been the official artist for the annual *Sturgis Motorcycle & Rally* magazine for the past six years, the only artist selected consecutively in the 60-year history of the event. His work has also been featured in other newspapers and magazines, including *Airbrush Action, Sunstorm, Art World News, ArtNews, US Art, VQ Magazine, American Iron, Easy Rider, Big Twin,* and *Iron Works* and on the covers of internationally recognized magazines such as the *Dupont Registry* and Chevy's *MidAmerica Catalog*. Scott's images have appeared in publications in Italy, Germany, Switzerland, Hong Kong, and around the world.

In 1998, Scott received a Vargas Award for his lifetime achievement in fine art. In addition to private collections, his work hangs in the permanent collection of L.A.'s Petersen's Museum, the L.A. County Museum, the St. Louis Museum, and the Milwaukee Museum.

Scott is represented by a Colorado-based publisher, Segal Fine Art. He recently relocated his studio and family from New Jersey to Southern California.

Even with a huge number of paintings already completed, there is no evidence that Scott is slowing down. Considering the growing demand for his originals, reproductions, and merchandise, there's little chance his fans would allow it.

BARBADOS
1990
30" x 40"
Acrylic on Belgian Linen
Collection of Rick and Cindy Jones

SEND IN THE CLOUDS
1990
30" x 40"
Acrylic on Belgian Linen
Collection of Dwayne McAninch

"Sometimes I put things in my paintings just to
see if anyone catches them, like the clouds in
the chrome of this 1959 Cadillac El Dorado that
don't appear in the sky."
SCOTT JACOBS

RUBY

1993
40" x 64"
Acrylic on Belgian Linen
Collection of Doug Adams

"When I started painting bikes, the Forbes Estate gave me full access to its collection. *Ruby* is a painting of the last bike Malcolm Forbes owned before he died in 1990."

SCOTT JACOBS

"*Ruby* is, without a doubt, one of the strongest pieces Scott has done. The original hangs behind the desk in my office, and I have the serigraphs displayed in the lobbies of my other offices in Chicago, Dallas, Charlotte, and Toronto."

DOUG ADAMS

Scott with the late
Malcolm S. Forbes, Sr.

13

CLEARED FOR TAKEOFF
1998
30" x 48"
Acrylic on Belgian Linen
Collection of Michael Jackson

From Scott's *Little Grownup* series
Scott photographed his neighbors
Joey and Delaney Roth for reference

IN SEARCH OF A RAINBOW
1990
30" x 40"
Acrylic on Belgian Linen
Collection of Rick and Cindy Jones

"I think Scott is far more than just a Harley artist. He has been
phenomenally successful with his Harleys and car paintings, but you have
to appreciate the whole scope of what he's done. The piece that gets the
most attention when anyone comes into our house is *In Search of a
Rainbow.* It's the one that grabs people by the throat and by the heart."

RICK JONES

OUTLAW
1993
28" x 42"
Acrylic on Belgian Linen
Collection unknown

CAUGHT IN A DAYDREAM

1998
36" x 48"
Acrylic on Belgian Linen
Collection of Kyle and Lori Mussman

"If you look closely, the initials of all the people
in this painting are carved in the wood."

SCOTT JACOBS

Scott's daughter, Alexa, posed for this piece,
along with Anthony Demich and Courtney
Hendrickson.

DON'T WORRY, I'LL SAVE YA

1998
32" x 40"
Acrylic on Belgian Linen
Collection of the artist

Cammy Demich and Zach Faust modeled
for *Don't Worry I'll Save Ya.*

THE FEARLESS

1992
20" x 20"
Acrylic on Masonite
Collection of Bill and Maggie Zures

"This picture of a fire truck in my hometown, my first photo-realistic painting, won first place in a local art contest."

SCOTT JACOBS

TO THE RESCUE

1994
22" x 30"
Acrylic on Linen
Collection of Scott Jacobs

"This is the local rescue squad in the town where I grew up."

SCOTT JACOBS

"When Harley-Davidson was deciding whether to license me as their official artist, they reviewed some of my paintings. After I showed them *'94 Special*, they made their final decision. It's an important piece for me."

SCOTT JACOBS

Signing an edition of
'94 Special prints

LIVE TO RIDE

1993
40" x 54"
Acrylic on Belgian Linen
Collection of Rick and Cindy Jones

"*Live to Ride* was my first piece produced as a print. The entire edition sold out in five weeks. The day before I went under contract with Segal Fine Art, Rick and Cindy Jones purchased the painting. It's really part of their collection, but they've never had possession of it, because it hangs in my living room. They bought it for me to enjoy."

SCOTT JACOBS

"When he was just starting out, Scott had this unfortunate but delightful problem—everything he painted sold in a heartbeat. I originally bought this painting so he would have something he could use to show his work. Over time, it has evolved into a signature piece, his first major release."

RICK JONES

MADE IN THE USA

1995
36" x 36"
Acrylic on Belgian Linen
Collection of Doug Adams

The artist's name makes a subliminal appearance in the speedometer of this Harley-Davidson Dyna Wide Glide.

"I started riding Harleys in 1995 and simultaneously discovered Scott's artwork. I've viewed a lot of other artists for Harley since then, and there's just nobody that compares to him."

DOUG ADAMS

FAT BOY

1993
30" x 40"
Acrylic on Belgian Linen
Collection unknown

"This is my first painting of a Harley."

SCOTT JACOBS

HERITAGE

1993
32" x 40"
Acrylic on Belgian Linen
Collection of Vincent Pacifico

"You can tell this is the original
painting because it's missing one
headlight visor. Three years after I
painted it, Segal Fine Art decided to
release a print, so I tracked down the
painting and added the missing visor."

SCOTT JACOBS

ROAD KING

1994
28" x 35"
Acrylic on Belgian Linen
Collection of Mel Gordon

"I photographed this 1994 Road King FLH the first time I went to Daytona Bike Week. It's the first bike I shot in Daytona."

SCOTT JACOBS

DRESSED TO THE NINES

1994
40" x 50"
Acrylic on Belgian Linen
Collection of Manfred Petritsch,
Harley-Davidson of Zug, Switzerland

"This is a painting of a Harley
Shovelhead owned by Bon Jovi
drummer Tico Torres."

SCOTT JACOBS

Scott and Bon Jovi drummer Tico Torres at the
Forbes Estate in New Jersey.

KING OF THE ROAD
1994
40" x 50"
Acrylic on Belgian Linen
Collection unknown

IRON STINGER

1994
28" x 42"
Acrylic on Belgian Linen
Collection of Vincent Pacifico

The artist's name makes another appearance; this time it's hidden on the carburetor cover.

INDIAN SUMMER

1994
36" x 48"
Acrylic on Belgian Linen
Collection of Mike Corbin

This is a 1953 Indian Chief.
"1953 was the last official
year for production of the
original Indian motorcycles."

SCOTT JACOBS

"I am a proud owner of a number of
Scott's original paintings. They bring a
great deal of beauty and enjoyment to
the lives of motorcycle lovers. Scott
possesses a way to illustrate the
common soul between motorcycle
and motorcyclist."

MIKE CORBIN

FLOWER POWER

1994
30" x 36"
Acrylic on Belgian Linen
Collection of CBS Records

"This bike was owned by a woman. I called
the painting *Flower Power* because the title,
like the piece itself, juxtaposes masculine
and feminine characteristics."

SCOTT JACOBS

'48 CHIEF
1994
40" x 40"
Acrylic on Belgian Linen
Collection of Mike Corbin

#9 DREAM

1994
40" x 40"
Acrylic on Belgian Linen
Collection of Joe Russo

"This was the 9th piece I did, and at the time I had a Fat Boy on order. It was my dream bike—hence the name, *#9 Dream.*"

SCOTT JACOBS

Experiencing a new kind of publicity, Arlen co-signs an entire print edition of *Awesome Ness* in Boulder, Colorado, with Scott.

"Scott really knows motorcycles—he gets every little detail, and his reflections are killer."
ARLEN NESS

AWESOME NESS

1994
36" x 64"
Acrylic on Belgian Linen
Collection of Arlen Ness

Designed and built by Arlen Ness, this
bike is the only one of its kind.

THE CHAMP

2000
32" x 40"
Acrylic on Belgian Linen
Collection of Paul Kegel

Scott Parker, nine time World
Champion

Scott with
Scott Parker,
No. 1 dirt track racer,
signing magazines in
Denver, 2000.

1938 1995

STURGIS

RALLY & RACES

SCOTT JACOBS

"INDIAN RACER   VINTAGE 1924"

INDIAN RACER
1995
30" x 44"
Acrylic on Belgian Linen
Collection of
Manfred Petritsch,
Harley-Davidson of Zug,
Switzerland

As artist for the world-renowned Sturgis Rally, Scott created the event's official poster, mingling images from several sources. The 1924 Indian Board Track Racer belonged to Steve McQueen. The composition was inspired by an original photo shot by photographer Jeff Hackett.

REFLECTIONS ON CANVAS

1995
36" x 48"
Acrylic on Belgian Linen
Collection of Mike Corbin

"The one thing people
remember about this painting of an
all-chrome Fat Boy is that no silver
paint was used. I named it after my
gallery in Westfield, New Jersey.
It seemed like the perfect title.
After all, it is reflections on canvas."

SCOTT JACOBS

Scott's annual show at
Reflections on Canvas, his
former gallery in New Jersey,
draws so many bikers that the
local police close the street.

'48 PANHEAD
1994
30" x 36"
Acrylic on Belgian Linen
Collection of David Holcomb

"People enjoy the farm scene
captured in the headlight."
SCOTT JACOBS

Thunder Row in progress

BUGATTI 1930 TYPE 50

1995
32" x 40"
Acrylic on Belgian Linen
Collection of Barry and Kim Cooney

"I traded this painting for
one-of-a-kind billet aluminum
wheels and tires for my Bentley."
SCOTT JACOBS

PREFERRED SEATING

1995
24" x 30"
Acrylic on Belgian Linen
Collection of Mike Corbin

PUMPING IRON
1995
40" x 46"
Acrylic on Belgian Linen
Collection of Dan Bree

"When I'm at Bike Week in Daytona, I walk around looking for bikes to paint. When I find one I like, I leave a note on the seat, explaining that I'm interested in doing a painting and asking the owner to come see me. My photographer, Jeff Hackett, set this shot at an old gas station in Daytona. The pumps don't work, but they've been kept for nostalgic reasons."
SCOTT JACOBS

Pumping Iron was reproduced on Scott's first licensed Harley-Davidson collector plate for the Franklin Mint.

Pumping Iron in progress. Starting with black paint, Scott creates basic shapes, then contrasts other colors against the black.

CATCH OF THE DAY

1995
48" x 56"
Acrylic on Belgian Linen
Collection of Bill Chaney,
Harley-Davidson of California

A 1968 Shovelhead on a dock on
the West Coast of Florida.

"I spent as much time on the back-
ground as I did on the motorcycle."
SCOTT JACOBS

PANACEA

1996
50" x 64"
Acrylic on Belgian Linen
Collection of Marshall Chesrown

A Harley-Davidson Panhead
at Daytona Bike Week

"Panacea: a cure for what ails you."
SCOTT JACOBS

PANACEA STUDY

1997
20" x 30"
Acrylic on Belgian Linen
Collection of Kyle and Lori Mussman

"The detail is just phenomenal—the
chrome shifter, the reflections, and the
lighting are all totally realistic. It jumps
off the canvas."

KYLE MUSSMAN

PANACEA STUDY #2

1999
11-1/4" x 16-1/2 "
Acrylic on Belgian Linen
Collection of Janice Dews

SAN FRAN PAN

1996
36" x 44"
Acrylic on Belgian Linen
Collection of Kyle and Lori Mussman

"It's a unique representation of the
'48 Panhead. I actually bought the
motorcycle and the painting."

KYLE MUSSMAN

The De Young Museum in
San Francisco opened its doors early and let
Scott and photographer Jeff Hackett bring
the bike in for a photo shoot.

SILVER LINING
1996
36" x 48"
Acrylic on Belgian Linen
Collection of
American Harley-Davidson,
Ann Arbor, Michigan

AMERICAN IRON

1996
26" x 16"
Watercolor on Illustration Board
Collection of Bill and Josie Chaney

From a photo taken by
photographer Don Rogers.

"This is my first watercolor painting."
SCOTT JACOBS

THE KING'S PALACE

1996
44" × 54"
Acrylic on Belgian Linen
Collection of Guy Edwards

Set in the Palace of
Fine Arts in San Francisco

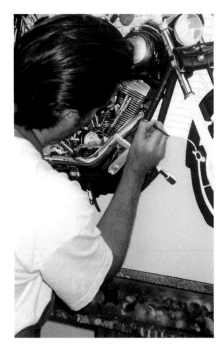

AMERICAN GRAFFITI
1997
36" x 48"
Acrylic on Belgian Linen
Collection of Vincent Pacifico

American Graffiti in progress

American Graffiti owner Vincent Pacifico snapped this picture of photographer Jeff Hackett shooting reference photos.

The first model, biker Tom Rogers, sat for about two hours on the side of Bear Butte Mountain in Sturgis, South Dakota.

A second model, Paul Heroux, donned a caveman outfit and posed in Scott's backyard for his stint.

"With this piece, I started with the title and built a painting around it. Some of the Harley motors built between 1984 and 1998 are referred to as the 'evolution engines.' I wanted to paint something I could call "*Evolution*," so I came up with this idea about a caveman carving the very first Harley."

SCOTT JACOBS

Left: The evolution of *Evolution*

The 1995 Fat Boy used as a reference for *Evolution*.

EVOLUTION
1996
48" x 62"
Acrylic on Belgian Linen
Collection of Dan Bishop

RENO NIGHTS
1995
40" x 54"
Acrylic on Belgian Linen
Collection of
Craig and Sandy Nicholas

"They closed off a street in
downtown Reno, Nevada, for four
hours so I could do this shoot.
They even kept the people away.
It gave me the ability to set up
the reflections the way I wanted."
SCOTT JACOBS

The palette for *Reno Nights*

Reno Nights in progress.

PURPLE HAZE

1996
28" x 40"
Acrylic on Belgian Linen

"I had this piece at a show, and a guy there loved it. Later, his wife came back to see it. She fell in love with it, too, and decided to buy it for her husband. Then she noticed the name of the painting— the words "Purple Haze" are printed on the license plate of her husband's bike. It was just meant to be."

SCOTT JACOBS

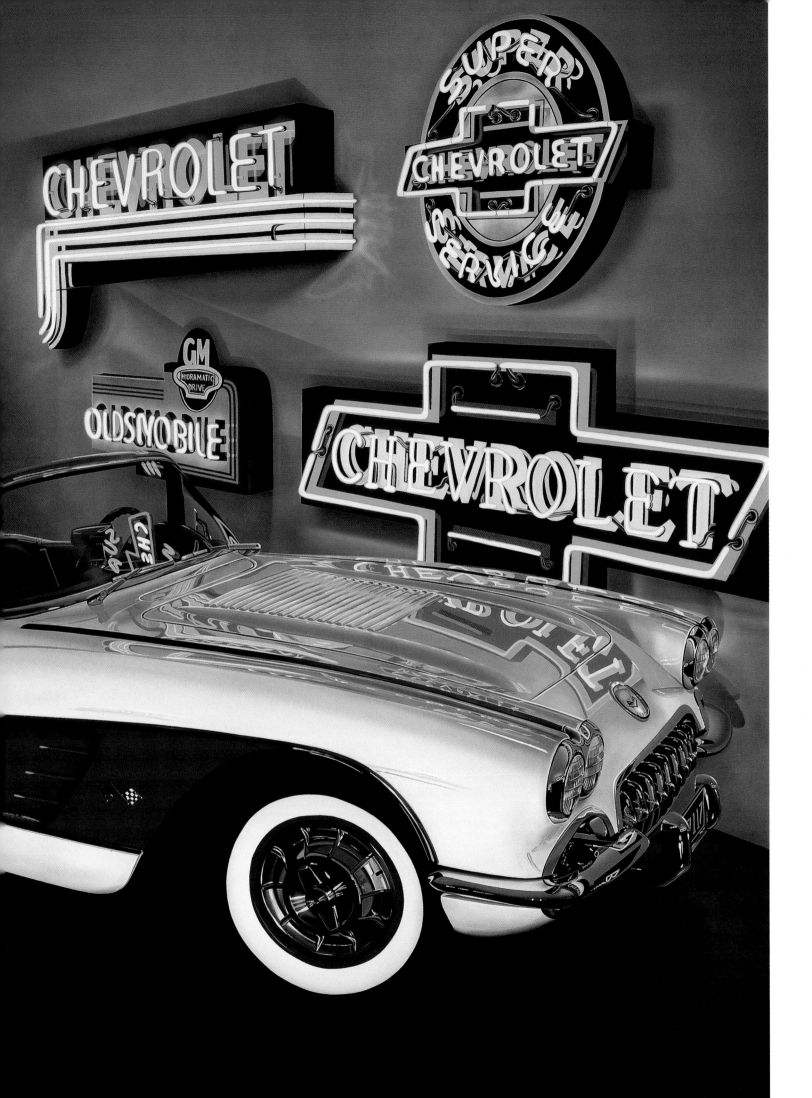

CHEZ'S DUELING DIABLOS
1997
50" x 64"
Acrylic on Belgian Linen
Collection of
Marshall Chesrown

Owner Marshall Chesrown had a Diablo motorcycle custom-made by Ron Simms to match his Lamborghini Diablo and commissioned Scott to paint a portrait of both vehicles.

'62 VETTE
1997
20" x 24"
Acrylic on Belgian Linen
Collection of Marshall Chesrown

"This is Marshall Chesrown's 1962 Corvette. I shot the reference photos while I was working on *Dueling Diablos*."

SCOTT JACOBS

1997
30" x 40"
Acrylic on Belgian Linen
Collection of Bill and Josie Chaney,
Harley-Davidson

The San Diego Automotive Museum
in Balboa Park, California, gave Scott
full access to its exotic bike collection.

"This was probably the most intense,
time-consuming small painting
I have ever done, because I had to
render all of the rough metal casings
and pits. Older bikes have more
exposed parts, compared to the
newer ones, which are encased."

SCOTT JACOBS

EENY-MEANY

1997
40" x 50"
Acrylic on Belgian Linen
Collection of Scott Jacobs

"The cars in this piece belong to a single family. I called the painting *Eeny Meany* because I figured when they go out in the morning, that's what they say when they're picking which car to drive."

SCOTT JACOBS

427

427

427

© Scott Jacobs

KYLE STYLE
1997
36" x 48"
Acrylic on Belgian Linen
Collection of Scott Jacobs

Scott with Kyle Petty's NASCAR at its inaugural race at Texas Motor Speedway.

KYLE'S HOT WHEELS

1997
36" x 48"
Acrylic on Belgian Linen
Collection of Mattel, Inc.

Kyle's Hot Wheels is displayed
in the reception area of Mattel's
corporate headquarters in
El Segundo, California.

Jeff Hackett, photographer

RIDE LIKE THE WIND

1998
36" x 48"
Acrylic on Belgian Linen
Collection of Kyle and Lori Mussman

A 1948 Panhead from the San Diego
Automotive Museum and the 1929
Stearman sightseeing plane that flies
daily over Scott's home.

SPLITTING IMAGE

1997
40" x 50"
Acrylic on Belgian Linen
Collection of Kyle and Lori Mussman

This Corvette was produced only in 1963 because its
split window obstructed the rear view.

C5

1997
32" x 40"
Acrylic on Belgian Linen
Collection of
Kyle and Lori Mussman

Produced for the cover
of the *DuPont Registry*.

CORVETTE

C5

HERITAGE II
1999
14-1/2" x 22"
Acrylic on Belgian Linen
Collection of Todd Erdman

SPRING FEVER

1998
36" x 48"
Acrylic on Belgian Linen
Collection of Bill and Josie Chaney,
Harley-Davidson

A 1998 Heritage Springer in
Ann Arbor, Michigan.

XL-ENT '57

1998
32" x 40"
Acrylic on Belgian Linen
Collection of Alex Brewer

The '57 XL, Harley's first Sportster.

ENDLESS SUMMER

1998
32" x 40"
Acrylic on Belgian Linen
Collection of Bruce and Kathy Jamieson

Collector Kathy Jamieson's Corvette on
the beach in Cardiff, California.

MOONSTRUCK

1998
26" x 36"
Acrylic on Belgian Linen
Collection of Scott Jacobs

This original 1998 Corvette C5 painting
has a place of honor in Scott's collection.

"I think everyone should have good art in
their laundry room."

SCOTT JACOBS

LIQUID STEEL

1998
32" x 36"
Acrylic on Belgian Linen
Collection of Tony DeCarlo

For a *Dupont Registry* cover: the first
liquid-cooled Porsche 996's.

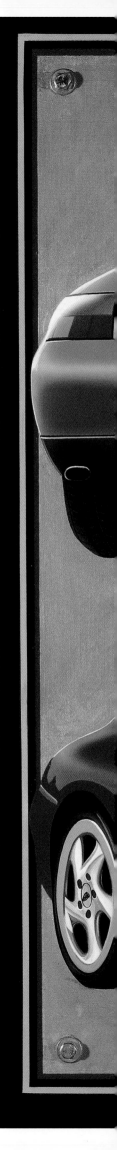

HAPPY
ANNIVERSARY
1998
38" x 55"
Acrylic on Belgian Linen
Collection of
Kyle and Lori Mussman

Celebrating
Harley-Davidson's
95th anniversary, this
painting was displayed in
the Milwaukee
Public Museum.

"You could get lost in the
details of this piece.
Scott's attention to detail
is far above and beyond
what I've seen from
other artists."

KYLE MUSSMAN

LOCOMOTION
2000
36" x 48"
Acrylic on Belgian Linen
Collection of Robert Steele,
Benjy's Harley-Davidson

A 1936 Knucklehead

INDIAN 80
1999
14" x 20"
Acrylic on Belgian Linen
Collection of Louis Gonzalez

AT YOUR SERVICE
1999
38" x 50"
Acrylic on Belgian Linen
Collection of
Kyle and Lori Mussman

1936 Knucklehead

HARLEY-DAVIDSON
SERVICE

CLASSIC '41

1999
32" x 50"
Acrylic on Belgian Linen
Collection of Roeder's Harley-Davidson

From the San Diego Automotive
Museum, a 1941 Knucklehead at the
entrance to Balboa Park.

THE NEW MILLENNIUM

1999
32" x 44"
Acrylic on Belgian Linen
Collection of Scott Jacobs

Harley's first 2000 model.

Take a closer look—some
additional images are hidden
among the rocks.

ROCK & ROLL
1999
30" x 40"
Acrylic on Belgian Linen
Collection of Scott Jacobs

Set in Joshua Tree State Park,
California, the only place in the
United States where
Joshua trees grow.

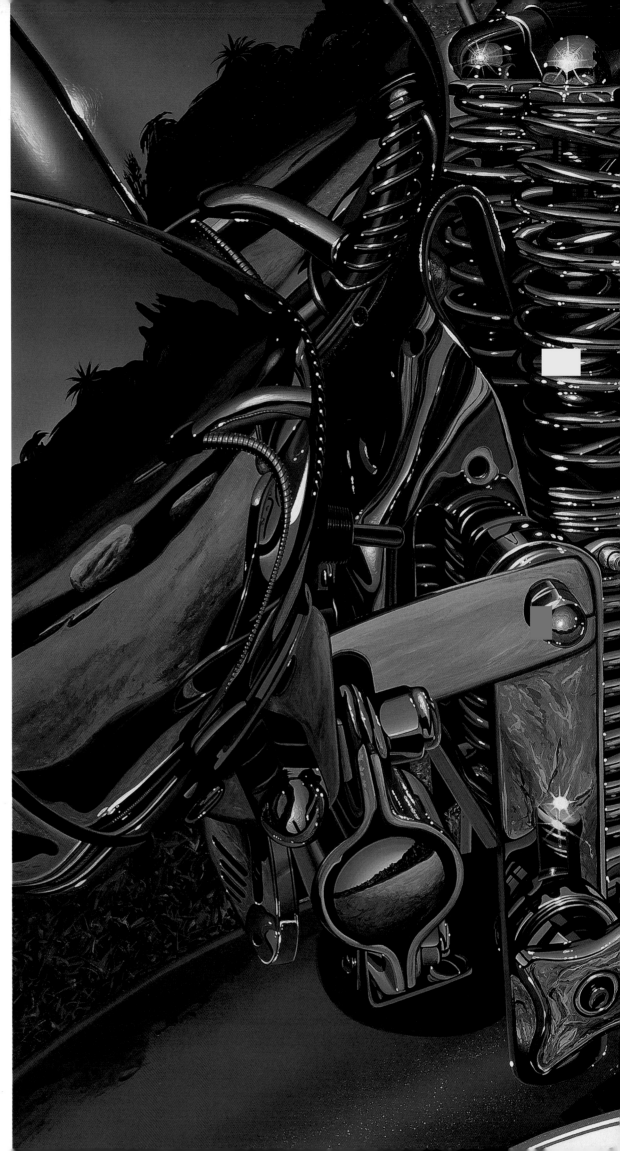

ABSTRACT WITH
HARLEY
2000
30" x 40"
Acrylic on Belgian Linen
Collection of
Doug and Susie Adams

108

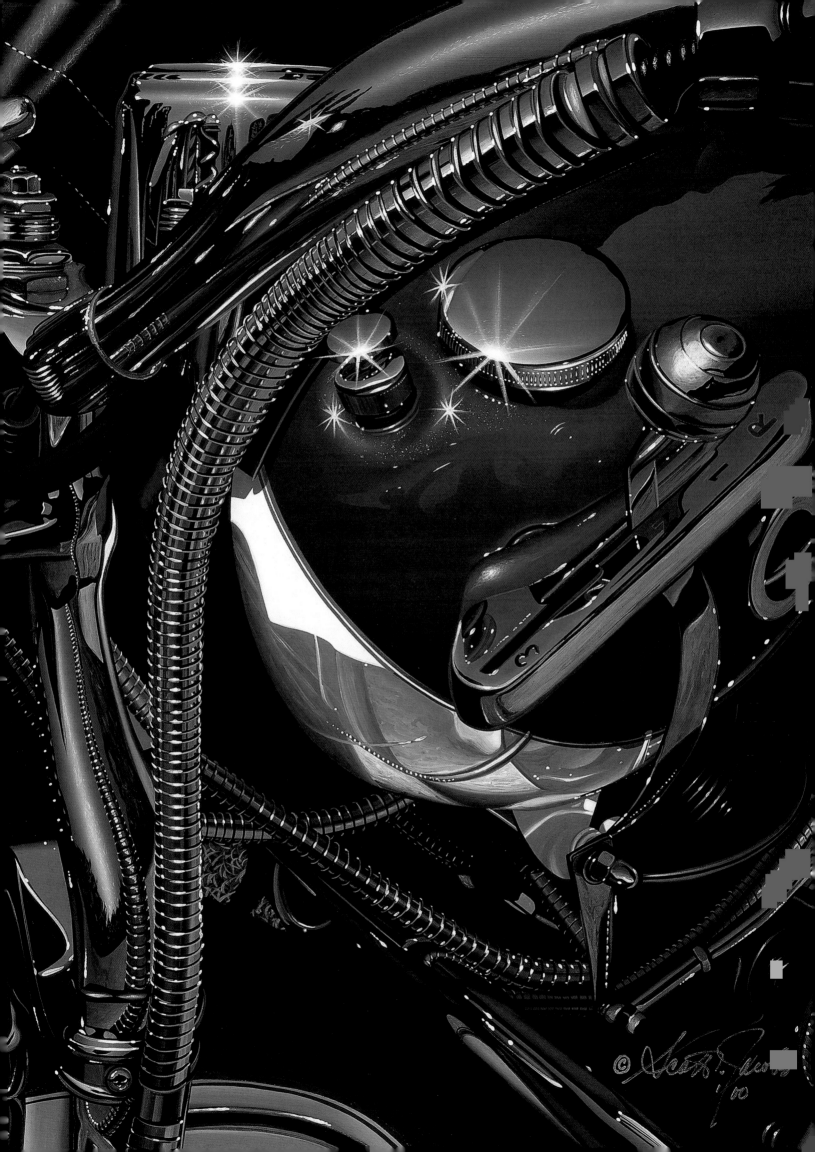

FAT BOY 2000

2000
36" x 48"
Acrylic on Belgian Linen
Collection of Stone Mountain
Harley-Davidson, Georgia

Parked outside an imaginary
restaurant, the three bikes pictured
here represent the lifespan of
the Harley-Davidson Fat Boy.
Restaurant signs reflect the relevant
years; the first model was produced
in 1990, and the two others in 2000.

BEST SEAT IN THE HOUSE
1999
16" x 20"
Acrylic on Belgian Linen
Collection of Scott Jacobs

1956 Corvette

FREEDOM
2000
36" x 48"
Acrylic on Belgian Linen
Collection of Scott Jacobs

A 1943 WLA and posters
from the same year.

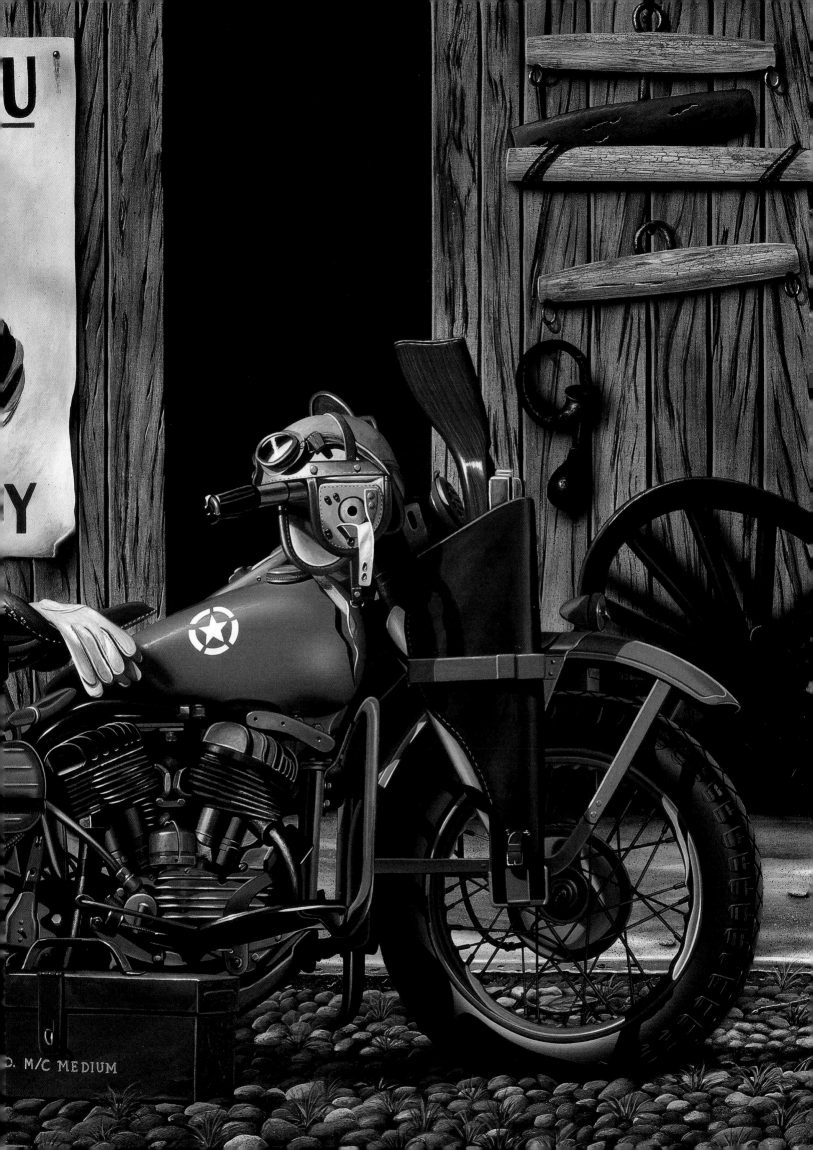

Playing drums with ZZ Top

Peter Fonda

Backstage with ZZ Top

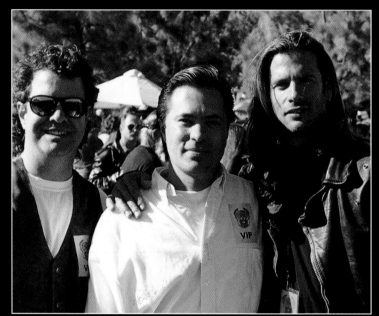
Ron Copple and Lorenzo Lamas

Nancy and Willie G. Davidson

Larry Hagman

Eva Herzigova

Jay Leno

Scott Parker at Sturgis

Joan Lunden

With rock band, Survivor

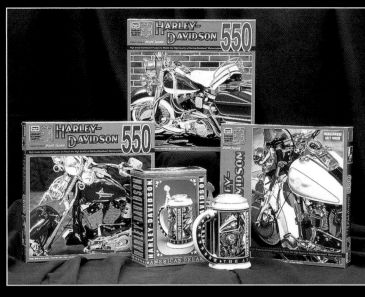

A small sampling of Jacobs licensed products available worldwide.

More than 100 international magazines have featured Scott's work.

INDEX

PRINTS, POSTERS AND REPRODUCTIONS

The items listed below are available for purchase.
For details, contact Segal Fine Art at
1(800) 999-1297 or visit their web site: www.segalfineart.com.

#9 Dream
Poster, T-shirt

'94 Special
Serigraph (paper)
T-shirt, Beer stein, Puzzles

At Your Service
Lithograph (paper), Giclee
(paper), T-shirt

Awesome Ness
Serigraph

Catch Of The Day
Lithograph (paper, canvas)
T-shirt, Tile, Plate

Caught in a Daydream
Giclee (paper, canvas)

Classic '41
Giclee (paper, canvas)

Cleared for Takeoff
Giclee (canvas)

Don't Worry, I'll Save Ya!
Giclee (paper)

Eeny-Meany
Lithograph, Giclee (canvas)

Endless Summer
Lithograph, Giclee (canvas)

Evolution
Giclee (paper), Poster

Fat Boy 2000
Giclee (paper, canvas)

Fearless
Lithograph (paper)

Fork It Over
Serigraph (paper,canvas)
T-shirt, Poster

Freedom
Giclee (paper, canvas)

Happy Anniversary
Lithograph (paper)
Giclee (paper), Tile

Indian Racer
Poster, T-shirt

Iron Stinger
Poster, T-shirt

King's Palace
Giclee (canvas), T-shirt
Plate

Knucklehead
Lithograph (paper, canvas)

Kyle's Hot Wheels
Poster, T-shirt

Live to Ride
Serigraph (paper)
T-shirt, Poster, Beer stein

Locomotion
Lithograph (canvas)

Look But Don't Touch
Serigraph (paper, canvas)
Beer stein

Made in the USA
Poster, T-shirt

New Millennium
Giclee (paper, canvas)

Moonstruck
Giclee (paper, canvas)

Neon Classic
Lithograph (paper)
Giclee (canvas), Clock

Panacea
Lithograph (paper,
canvas), T-shirt, Tile

Pumping Iron
Lithograph (paper, canvas)
T-shirt, Plate

Reflections on Canvas
Poster, T-shirt

Reno Nights
Lithograph (paper, canvas)
T-shirt

Ride Like the Wind
Lithograph (paper, canvas)
T-shirt

Road King
Poster, T-shirt

Ruby
Serigraph (paper)
T-shirt, Puzzles

San Fran Pan
Giclee (canvas), T-shirt

Splitting Image
Lithograph (paper)
Giclee (canvas)

Spring Fever
Giclee (canvas), T-shirt

Thunder Row
Serigraph (paper, canvas)
T-shirt, Tile

The Champion
Lithograph (canvas)